HAPPY EVER CRAFTER

KNIGHTS AND CASTLES

ANNALEES LIM

WAYLAND
www.waylandbooks.co.uk

First published in Great Britain in 2018 by Wayland
Copyright © Hodder and Stoughton 2018

Senior Commissioning Editor: Melanie Palmer
Design: Square and Circus
Illustrations: Supriya Sahai

Additional illustrations: Freepik

HB ISBN 978 1 5263 0753 8
PB ISBN 978 1 5263 0754 5

Printed in China

Wayland
An imprint of
Hachette Children's Group
Part of Hodder and Stoughton
Carmelite House
50 Victoria Embankment
London EC4Y 0DZ

An Hachette UK Company
www.hachette.co.uk

SAFETY INFORMATION:
Please ask an adult for help with any activities
that could be tricky, involve cooking or handling
glass. Ask adult permission when appropriate.

Due care has been taken to ensure the activities
are safe and the publishers regret they cannot
accept liability for any loss or injuries sustained.

CONTENTS

Knights and Castles

Heroic knights upon noble steeds were a common sight between the 5th and 15th century, a period of time in Europe known as The Middle Ages. As new kingdoms were formed, royal families would grant knighthoods to people wishing to serve as warriors who pledged to protect and defend the monarchy, the poor and the religion they believed in.

To become a knight you had to be a great horse rider, have excellent sword wielding skills, and most importantly you had to be wealthy enough to buy your own armour, weapons and horse. But don't worry, you can easily become a knight without having to trade in your treasures. In this book you will find simple crafty makes and party ideas made from lots of recycled materials and things you find from around the house. It won't be long until you have made all the things you need to go out and complete your medieval quests.

The legend of King Arthur is probably one of the most famous stories about this period of time, but it is still not known if Arthur was a real person or not. Tales of his reign have been told many different times over the centuries but the stories all include his wife Guinevere, Merlin the Wizard, his sword Excalibur, and of course The Knights of the Round Table.

FACT!

The tale of **George and the Dragon** is so famous all around the world that England, Portugal, Georgia, Lithuania and Greece made him their patron saint.

FACT!

The word knight is often thought to mean a person who is brave and chivalrous but it actually comes from an old English word for servant.

TOP TIP

Recycling and reusing unwanted things is a great way to make your craft project environmentally friendly. Always wash old food containers or fabric before you start using them. You can also collect old envelopes, birthday cards and cardboard boxes instead of buying reams of new paper. Don't forget to ask an adult before you take anything you see lying around the house – it might not be ready for the recycling bin just yet!

KINGDOM OF COSTUMES

Dressing up in a costume is a great way to feel like you have travelled back to a different time. Medieval clothes might be very different from today's fashion but it's easy to recreate them with these simple costume ideas.

KNIGHT'S ARMOUR

Knights would wear full plate armour made from iron or steel which means it was really heavy, protecting them from swords and spears. Try this helmet on for size, which is not only lightweight but will make you look the part, too.

YOU WILL NEED:
- LARGE PLATE • PENCIL • SCISSORS
- CARDBOARD/THICK CARD
- STICKY TAPE
- PAINT • PAINTBRUSH

1. Draw around a large plate on to some cardboard and cut out.

2. Cut out a long piece of card that is at least 30 cm tall and long enough wrap around the card circle and cut slits into the top.

3. Cut out a hole from the front and bend the slits down.

4. Stick the long piece of card on to the circle with tape. Add a cardboard diamond to the top, too.

5. Paint grey and add details in black.

PRINCESS CONE HAT

These tall headdresses, called *hennin*, were worn by royalty and the rich people of the time. Most were usually about 45 cm tall but some were even taller, at around 80 cm. They were traditionally made from a wire mesh covered in a light fabric, but this craft can be made from painted recycled card and tissue paper.

YOU WILL NEED:
- CARDBOARD (YOU CAN TAPE LOTS OF PIECES OF FLATTENED FOOD PACKAGING TOGETHER TO MAKE IT BIG ENOUGH) • RULER
- SCISSORS • PENCIL • PAINT • PAINTBRUSH • HOLE PUNCH
- STICKY TAPE • STRING OR RIBBON • TISSUE PAPER

1. Cut out a quarter circle shape from the card. The length of the straight edges will be how high the hat will be.

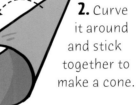

2. Curve it around and stick together to make a cone.

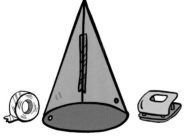

3. Punch a hole either side of the bottom of the cone.

TOP TIP
If you don't have tissue paper, cut up strips of white or clear plastic bags and stick them to the top of the cone instead.

4. Paint the cone in one colour, but add details at the bottom to make a decorative rim.

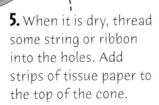

5. When it is dry, thread some string or ribbon into the holes. Add strips of tissue paper to the top of the cone.

SHIELD

Shields come in different shapes and the way they are decorated shows which army or side the knight belonged to, which was useful in battle. They were worn on the arm and helped protect the knights during attacks.

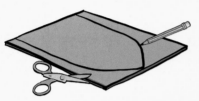

1. Draw a shield shape on to the cardboard and cut out.

2. Cut two strips of card and stick them on to the back with tape.

3. Decorate the shield with the scrap pieces of cardboard and stick in place with craft glue.

4. Paint the shield in lots of colours and leave to dry.

5. Dip the brush in a dark coloured paint and wipe most of it off on to some scrap paper or card. Lightly paint over the shield to make it look worn from battle. This technique is called *dry brushing*.

DID YOU KNOW?
A round shield is called a **Buckler**, a teardrop shaped shield is called a **Kite** and the one in this craft is called a **Heater**.

BOW AND ARROW

Archers used bows and arrows in battle or to hunt animals but today we use them mainly for sport, aiming them at targets in archery.

YOU WILL NEED:

- WIRE COAT HANGER • STRING
- MASKING TAPE • PAINT
- PAINTBRUSH • COLOURED CARD
- SCISSORS • WHITE CRAFT GLUE
- WOODEN SKEWERS

1. Bend a wire coat hanger into a curve. If an adult has wire cutters, ask them to remove the hook, but this is not essential.

2. Tie some string to the wire before wrapping masking tape around so that it makes a solid shape.

3. Paint the bow and leave to dry.

TOP TIP

You can also make this craft using any curved sticks you find when you are out walking in a park. Use any straight sticks you find for the arrows.

4. Cut out four feather shapes and two triangle shapes from coloured card.

5. Fold the feather shapes before sticking them on to the top of the wooden skewers. Then glue the triangles on to cover the other end.

9

KING OF THE CASTLE

Make your party the best celebration in the land by planning it all to perfection. Use the top tips and make all you need to entertain your fellow adventurous knights and merry maidens, creating your very own medieval world with decoration ideas, themed craft projects and more.

GET STARTED
Don't run out of time to make all the things you need for your party. Making a list is a really easy and quick way to help you remember all the important things you need to do.

 1. Find a venue Whether you are planning a birthday party or a holiday celebration, you will need to find a place to host your guests. Remember to decorate the space with the ideas you will find on page 16 to create your own themed kingdom.

 2. Joking Around Jesters were a traditional way to keep guests happy but you won't need to hire anyone to entertain the people at your party. Use the game ideas on page 12 to keep the fun going for hours.

 3. Fantastic Feasts Banquets were common in medieval times, with lots of food and drink served on long tables. There are lots of simple recipes on page 20 that are so delicious that your guests will be piling their plates high.

 4. Perfect Presents Make prizes for the games you play, extra decorations for your themed room, or presents for your guests to say thank you for coming to your party. Turn to page 24 for lots of ideas.

 5. Medieval Materials Write a list of everything you need. A lot of the craft projects in this book can be made from recycled materials. Save scrap paper, old food containers and upcycle things you were going to throw away. Thinking creatively will save you money, and you will help to save the planet, too.

HEAR YE, HEAR YE!

Town criers used to read from scrolls to shout announcements to the public, spreading important news. Making these scroll invitations is a great way to invite all the guests on your list, and has all the information they need to know.

To:
Write the name of your guest

Where:
The address of the party

When:
The time and date of the party

Dress code:
Suggest what people should wear to your party

RSVP:
Ask people to let you know if they can come

Greetings

To:

Where:

When:

Dress code:

RSVP:

MEDIEVAL MADNESS

These party games might not be traditional but they are fun to make and play. Each one of these games has simple instructions to follow and can be changed to make each project personalised by using different colours, patterns and designs.

GRAB THE FLAGS

Flags and banners decorated the great halls of the royal castles. They would hang from the walls and ceiling and all had their own pictures on called a coat of arms. These symbols were unique to one family, so you always knew whose house you were in.

YOU WILL NEED:

- PAPER (ABOUT A4 IN SIZE)
- SCISSORS • COLOURED PENS

HOW TO PLAY

Hide the flags around the room. Race against other players or teams to collect all the flags of the same colour. The fastest team or player wins.

1. Fold a rectangular piece of paper in half.

2. Cut a 'V' shape into the opposite end of the fold.

3. Draw your coat of arms picture on to the front. Repeat until you have 5 identical flags.

4. Make a set of flags in different colours for each player or number of teams you have.

FACE THE FOOLS

Court jesters were good at acrobatics, juggling, telling jokes and doing magic tricks, always doing their best to make people smile. Challenge your pals to a competition and try not to laugh as you pull the silliest faces to turn those frowns upside down.

YOU WILL NEED:

- SCISSORS • GLUE STICK
- STICKY TAPE • COLOURED PENS
- COLOURED PAPER • THICK CARD
- THIN CARD (OR PAPER PLATE)

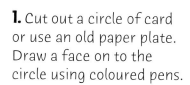

1. Cut out a circle of card or use an old paper plate. Draw a face on to the circle using coloured pens.

2. Make a hat, collar and circle bells using colourful paper or thin card.

3. Cut out a handle using some thick card. Decorate by drawing on some diamond shapes.

4. Stick all the pieces together to make the mask. Repeat the steps so that everyone can make their own.

HOW TO PLAY

Two people play this game at a time and sit opposite each other. Both players hold up a mask so it covers their face. They make a silly face behind it and on the count of three, reveal their face. The first to laugh loses the game and the winner goes on to challenge the next person.

CHAINED UP

Medieval shackles were used in dungeons to keep prisoners locked up if they had committed crimes. They were made from steel so were heavy to wear and almost impossible to escape from.

YOU WILL NEED:

- ELASTIC BANDS • PAPER (MAGAZINE PAGES ARE IDEAL) • STAPLER • RULER
- PENCIL • SCISSORS

1. Cut up 5 small lengths of paper that are 15 cm x 5 cm in size.

2. Thread one elastic band on to one piece of paper and staple into a circle. Repeat so that you have two in total.

3. Join the two paper circles with more lengths of paper stapled into circles.

4. Repeat so that you have enough for the amount of people playing. Each person playing will need one chain.

HOW TO PLAY

Stand in a small circle. Each person puts a chain into their right hand and reaches into the middle. Everyone puts their left hand into the other end of the chain of someone that is standing opposite. The aim of the game is to untangle everyone so that you are all standing in a circle without removing or breaking the chains.

JOUSTING TOURNAMENT

YOU WILL NEED:
- NEWSPAPER • GLUE STICK
- SCISSORS • THICK CARD
- PAPER CUPS • PAINT • PAINTBRUSH

Medieval jousting was a popular test of skill and courage. People wearing armour rode horses towards each other with long spears called lances and tried to be the first to strike the other.

1. Open out a piece of newspaper and spread some glue on to the edges. Roll the unglued side into a tight tube until you reach the opposite edge.

2. Open out another piece of newspaper and spread some glue on two edges. Roll up the original tube inside the newspaper to make a fatter tube. Repeat three or four times for each lance.

3. Cut out a circle from some thick card. Cut a hole in the middle of the circle so it slides up the lance.

4. Make the targets by sticking card rings on to an upside down paper cup.

5. Decorate the targets and the lances with paint.

HOW TO PLAY
Place the targets on to a table or chair each. The two players stand facing their target, about ten paces back. After the count of three, the players run towards the targets. The winner is the fastest to catch the target and hook it on to their lance.

PARTY DECORATIONS

Transform your home into a fancy fort, filled with decorations inspired by medieval times. Cover walls, tables or even hang them from the ceiling to give your party space a makeover, ready for your castle-themed celebrations.

COAT OF ARMS

A knight's armour would cover his whole body, including his face, so it was hard to tell who was who. A coat of arms was designed for each knight with different pictures, writing and symbols so that each one was unique. This would be worn over the armour, like a badge (or coat), and also on their flags and banners, too.

1. Draw a design on to a piece of paper. Try to include some animals, a shield and flags.

2. Cut out each element carefully so that you have lots of templates to draw around.

YOU WILL NEED:

- PAPER • PENCIL • SCISSORS
- OLD T-SHIRT • WOODEN STICK
- STRING • FELT-TIP PENS

TOP TIP

With an adult, search the internet to see if your surname has a coat of arms linked to it. You could use this as inspiration for your design.

3. Fold the t-shirt in half and cut two lines to make the flag shape.

4. Use the paper templates to draw the design on to the fabric using felt-tip pens.

5. Thread a wooden stick through the sleeves and tie string or ribbon on to the sides, so it can be hung up.

FLYING DRAGONS

Tales of fierce dragons guarding precious treasures were popular in medieval times and often appeared in lots of artwork. One of the most popular tales was of Saint George and the Dragon. He rescued a princess from a dragon and saved a whole town, too.

YOU WILL NEED:

- TWO PLASTIC MILK CARTONS • GREEN TISSUE PAPER/MAGAZINE PAGES
- WHITE CRAFT GLUE • PAPER • PENCIL
- SCISSORS • PAINT • PAINTBRUSH

2. Tear up pieces of green tissue paper or magazine pages and glue them on to the cartons. Leave to dry.

1. Tape together two plastic milk cartons.

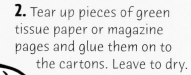

Why was King Arthur's army too tired to fight?
Because they had a few sleepless knights.

3. Cut out some ears, eyes, wings, legs, a tail and scales from coloured paper.

4. Paint a nose, and mouth and scales.

5. Stick on the cut out paper to the body using more craft glue.

TOP TIP

Make the dragon soar through the air by tying string to the body and hanging it up.

TOURNAMENT TENTS

Knights would use tents to sleep in during their long expeditions or at large events like jousting tournaments. They were often round and very colourful with lots of flags and bunting hanging from them.

YOU WILL NEED:
- A4 PAPER • FELT-TIP PENS
- PENCIL • SCISSORS • STICKY TAPE

1. Cut out a long strip of paper (about half the size of A4) and fold it into 6 equal pieces.

2. Draw three quarters of a circle on to a piece of paper, draw triangles all around the edge and cut out.

4. Stick the paper strip together to make a hexagon shape and fold the circle together to make a cone.

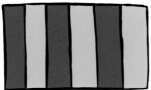

3. Colour in the circle and paper strip using felt-tip pens.

5. Cut a slit halfway up one of the hexagon sides to make the opening of the tent, and add some more flags to the outside.

TOP TIP
Make lots of these tents in different colours and use them to decorate your banquet table. You can make them in different sizes, too!

CASTLE AND DRAWBRIDGE

Medieval castles were built with tall, strong walls and were often surrounded by water to keep enemies out. When the drawbridge was up, it was used as a big door to seal off the entrance, but when it was lowered it was used as a bridge so that you could cross the water.

1. Tape down the lids of 4 fizzy drinks cans. Cover in paper and draw on some windows and bricks.

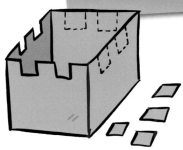

2. Cut squares out from the top of the cardboard box and decorate the outside with windows and bricks.

YOU WILL NEED:
- 4 FIZZY DRINKS CANS • PAPER
- SCISSORS • CARDBOARD BOX
- STICKY TAPE • THICK CARD
- STRING • FELT-TIP PENS

3. Cut the same size squares from the tops of four strips of thick card and stick these on to the top of the cans.

4. Make the door by cutting a rectangle from one side of the cardboard box, then cut off all four corners.

5. Make a drawbridge from more thick card and use string to attach it to the castle. Stick the turrets into the corners, too.

FANTASTIC FEASTS

Entertaining guests at fine banquets was a common medieval pastime. Tasty food was presented in a fancy way on The Great Table for the most important people. Impress your guests with these delicious recipes.

CASTLE TOWERS

Castle towers were often round so that you could see out in all directions and spot any enemies approaching. They had small windows so that arrows could be fired out and they also protected you from any incoming attacks.

YOU WILL NEED:
- PAPER • CARDBOARD BOX
- STICKY TAPE • SCISSORS
- FELT-TIP PENS
- COOKED POPCORN

1. Wrap some paper loosely around a cardboard box and tape in place.

2. Fold one end, as if you were wrapping a present and tape it down.

TOP TIP
Try making mint chocolate chip flavoured popcorn! Mix a spoonful of honey with some mint extract flavouring and dark chocolate chips in a big bowl. Add the popcorn and coat evenly in the mixture before serving.

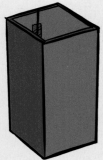

3. Remove the box so you end up with a paper bag.

4. Cut out squares from the top and decorate to look like a tower.

5. Fill with popcorn and serve.

FLAMING TORCHES

As the lightbulb was not invented until 1879, homes were only lit up by candlelight and fires before this time. Torches were often used in castles and mounted along the walls or held by hand to light the way.

YOU WILL NEED:
- VANILLA ICE CREAM • ICE CREAM CONE
- MANGO • PINEAPPLE • KNIFE
- A STRAWBERRY • WHITE CHOCOLATE
- ORANGE FOOD COLOURING

1. With an adult, cut up some mango and pineapple slices into triangles.

2. Mix together white chocolate and some drops of orange food colouring.

3. Put a scoop of vanilla ice cream into an ice cream cone.

4. Drizzle the orange chocolate over the top.

5. Stick a strawberry into the middle of the ice cream and put the mango and pineapple slices around it.

FLAG COOKIES

This is a great activity to involve your friends with the celebrations. Everyone gets a cookie to decorate and makes their own design. Use this project as a starting point and let your imagination do the rest.

YOU WILL NEED:

- BISCUITS OR COOKIES • SWEETS
- ICING PENS • WATER ICING
- FOOD COLOURING
- GREASEPROOF PAPER • PEN

1. Draw a flag outline using icing pens.

2. Use different coloured icing to fill in the shapes.

3. Press some sweets in the middle and leave to set for a few minutes.

4. Draw the rest of the patterns on to the top using the icing pens.

5. Display them on a sheet of greaseproof paper, with flagpoles drawn on.

Why could you never find St George around in the daytime?

Because he went to knight school!

SAVOURY AXES

Battle axes were popular weapons before being replaced by gunpowder in the 16th century. They were mostly made of iron or steel with a wooden handle and crafted by hand by the local blacksmith.

YOU WILL NEED:

- PUFF PASTRY • ROLLING PIN
- TIN FOIL • KNIFE • PAPER
- SCISSORS • PEN • TOMATO SAUCE
- PEPPERS • CHEESE • BREADSTICKS

1. Fold a piece of paper in half and draw on a simple axe shape, then cut out.

2. Roll out the ready made puff pasty so that it is about 1 cm thick.

3. Use the template to cut out the axe head shapes from the pastry.

20 MINUTES

5. Press down the edges so that the mixture is sealed in and bake for 20 minutes at a medium heat.

4. Cover one half of the axe head with a layer of tomato sauce, chopped peppers and cheese. Place the breadstick in the middle and fold over the other half.

TOP TIP

Cover the breadstick handle in tin foil before you bake it so that it does not burn.

MEDIEVAL MAKES

Gather all your junk materials and transform them into toys, gifts and prizes. Why not invite your friends round for a crafting party and ask them to bring any spare materials they have, too.

CASTLE CASH

Bartering was a popular way to get the things you wanted by exchanging one thing for another. But as towns and villages grew, people used coins as a way to buy things. You would mostly find silver coins in medieval times, with gold only appearing later as new mines were discovered.

YOU WILL NEED:
- 1 CUP OF SALT • 2 CUPS OF FLOUR
- ¾ CUP WATER • SILVER PAINT
- PAINTBRUSH • THICK CARD
- SCISSORS • PENCIL • WHITE CRAFT GLUE • PERMANENT MARKER PEN

1. Cut out a circle of card and decorate with pieces of cut card to make a stamp.

2. Mix the salt, flour and water together to make the dough. Add more water or flour if necessary.

3. Roll small bits into balls and press them flat using the card stamp.

1 HOUR

4. Bake at a low heat for about an hour, or until they have dried out completely.

5. Paint the coins silver and leave to dry before adding any extra details on with a permanent marker pen.

TOP TIP
Make a coin pouch by cutting out a circle of fabric and punching holes round the edge. Thread some ribbon through the holes and gather together to make the pouch.

CATAPULT

During medieval times, catapults were large wooden weapons that threw heavy objects, arrows or stones great distances. As defences grew better over the years, the catapult became less useful in battles.

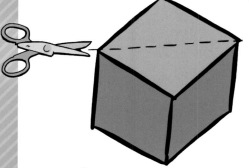

YOU WILL NEED:

- CARDBOARD BOX • PENCIL
- SCISSORS • ELASTIC BAND
- PLASTIC SPOON • STICKY TAPE
- SCRAP PAPER

1. Cut the cardboard box in half so you have a triangle base.

2. Cut a wide slit up one side and make hole with a pencil at the top and the bottom of the triangle.

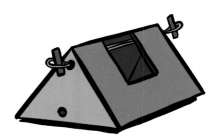

4. Put a pencil through the bottom two holes and tape a plastic spoon to the middle.

3. Thread an elastic band through the top two holes and keep it taught by holding it in place with a piece of cardboard each side.

5. Keep the spoon upright by putting it inbetween the elastic band.

HOW TO PLAY

Pull the spoon back, fill with some scrunched paper and let go to launch.

25

SWORD IN THE STONE

The tale of the 'Sword in the Stone' is one of many stories about King Arthur. People from far and wide came to try and remove the magical sword that was stuck in the stone. Everyone failed except a young boy called Arthur, who was then crowned the King of England.

1. Cut out a sword shape from thick card.

2. Wrap tin foil around the top to make it silver, and mould more around the bottom to make the handle 3D.

3. Scrunch up a ball of newspaper around tip of the sword and tape the ball together.

4. Remove the sword and wrap more foil around the ball of newspaper, keeping a gap for the sword to go in.

5. Paint the stone and the sword handle with acrylic paint.

DID YOU KNOW?
'The Lady of the Lake' is an alternative story about how King Arthur came to own his sword, Excalibur. In this story, King Arthur is given the sword by a mysterious and magical lady from the lake.

PHONE THRONE

Medieval royalty sat on large thrones, often made from wood with high backs and fancy decorations. They were positioned up high, so that they would be seen as the most important person in the room.

YOU WILL NEED:
- CARDBOARD BOX (OLD MEDICINE BOTTLE PACKAGING IS PERFECT) • SCISSORS
- GLUE STICK • PAINT • PAINTBRUSH
- BLACK MARKER PEN

1. Cut the box in half then cut the front and top off one of the halves.

2. Stick the two halves together with glue.

3. Paint the whole thing brown to look like wood and leave to dry.

4. Decorate with paint. Use a black marker pen to add some more details.

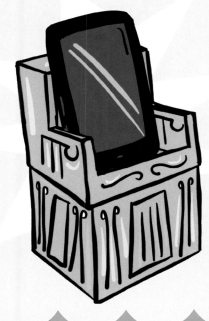

5. Cut a square of fabric and place it in the seat of the throne.

MINI KNIGHTS

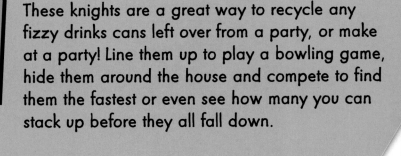

These knights are a great way to recycle any fizzy drinks cans left over from a party, or make at a party! Line them up to play a bowling game, hide them around the house and compete to find them the fastest or even see how many you can stack up before they all fall down.

YOU WILL NEED:

- FIZZY DRINKS CANS • TIN FOIL
- GLUE STICK • SCISSORS • CARD
- COLOURED PAPER • STICKY TAPE

1. Tape down the lid of the can. Cover the middle of the can with a strip of tin foil.

2. Cut out two arms, a semi circle and a sword from the card.

3. Cover these with tin foil, too.

4. Make a colourful shield from the coloured paper and stick to the middle of the can.

5. Cut out a face and arms from the paper and stick to the can along with the other silver pieces.

JOUSTING PENCIL TOPPER

As well as being a popular sport, jousting also acted like a court of law. The winner of a jousting competition or tournament would be deemed not guilty of any crime as they were seen to have God on their side.

YOU WILL NEED:
- PENCIL • PAPER • SCISSORS
- COLOURED PENS • GLUE STICK

1. Fold a piece of paper in half and make 2 small slits into the folded edge.

2. Open this up and draw a horse shape, then it cut out.

3. Fold another piece of paper in half and draw a knight.

4. Cut this out, remembering to cut slits for the arms.

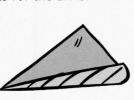

5. Roll up another piece of paper for the lance.

6. Stick the paper parts on to the pencil. Stick the lance under the arm. Bend the other arm to the front.

What is the name of a knight who likes to jump out on people?
Sir Prize!

JESTER JUGGLING BALLS

Medieval jugglers would earn their money by performing to people at fairs and market squares. Unlike the jesters at court who were only employed by the king or the rich, these jugglers were like the street performers of today and would entertain anyone that passed by.

YOU WILL NEED:

- BALLOONS • SCRAP PAPER • STICKY TAPE • SCISSORS • SCRAP FELT OR FABRIC • SAND/RICE • WHITE CRAFT GLUE

RICE

3. Knot the open end of the balloon so that there are no leaks.

1. Roll the piece of paper into a cone, taping it in place before cutting off the pointed end.

2. Place the cone into the neck of the balloon and fill with the sand or rice.

4. Draw and cut out the face and clothes from scrap felt of fabric.

5. Stick the fabric decorations on to the balloon using the white craft glue. Leave to dry completely before using them to juggle.

TOP TIP

Its easier to learn to juggle with just 3 balls and it's a good idea to make them all the same size and weight.

ROYAL PUPPETS

The medieval period lasted over 400 years so there were lots of different leaders during that time. Strict rules meant that all those who ruled were male. Empress Matilda was the only surviving heir to the throne in 1135, but she was prevented from taking the crown and her cousin, Stephen of Blois, was chosen instead.

1. Stuff some scrap fabric into the top of the sock and place the stick inside the sock, too.

2. Secure the scrap fabric in place with an elastic band so it makes a ball.

YOU WILL NEED:

- SOCK • SCRAP FABRIC
- ELASTIC BANDS • SCISSORS
- PAPER CUP • WOODEN STICK OR SKEWER • FABRIC GLUE

3. Make a hole in the middle of the paper cup and put the stick through it.

4. Place the sock around the edge of the cup and hold in place using another elastic band.

5. Decorate the puppet with scrap fabric to make the face, hair, arms, clothes and a crown.

KNIGHTS PUZZLE
CAN YOU FIND THE ANSWERS TO THESE QUESTIONS?

1. Which Knight does not have a belt buckle?

2. How many flags can you count in the picture?

3. Which knight has a different weapon to the others?

4. Can you spot which knight has different shoes?

ANSWERS 1. B 2. 8 flags 3. A 4. C

DISCOVER MORE...

HAPPY EVER CRAFTER

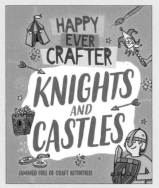

978 1 5263 0753 8

Realm of Knights and Castles
Kingdom of Costumes
King of the Castle
Invitations
Party Games
Party Decorations
Fantastic Feasts
Medieval Makes
Knights Puzzle

978 1 5263 0755 2

Sci-Fi Worlds
Outer Space Outfits
Planet Party
Intergalactic Invites
Party Games
Party Decorations
Space Food
Crafty Makes
Space Puzzle

978 1 5263 0751 4

Once Upon a Time
Costumes and Characters
Enchanted Accessories
Invitations
Party Games
Party Food
Party Decorations
Crafty Makes
Fairy Puzzle

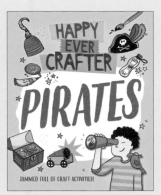

978 1 5263 0713 2

Argh M' Hearties!
Daring Dressing Up
Pirate Plans
Invitations
Party Games
Party Decorations
Party Food
Crafty Makes
Pirate Puzzle

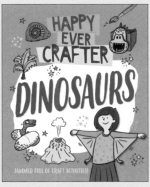

978 1 5263 0757 6

Dinosaur World
Big Beasts Fancy Dress
Prehistoric Party Plans
Invitations
Party Games
Party Decorations
Party Food
Craft-o-saurus
Dinosaur Puzzle

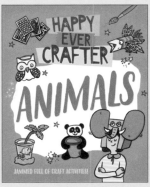

978 1 5263 0759 0

Amazing Animals
Cute Creature Costumes
Party Animal
Invitations
Party Games
In the Zoo
Tasty Treats
Creature Crafts
Animals Puzzle

WAYLAND
www.waylandbooks.co.uk

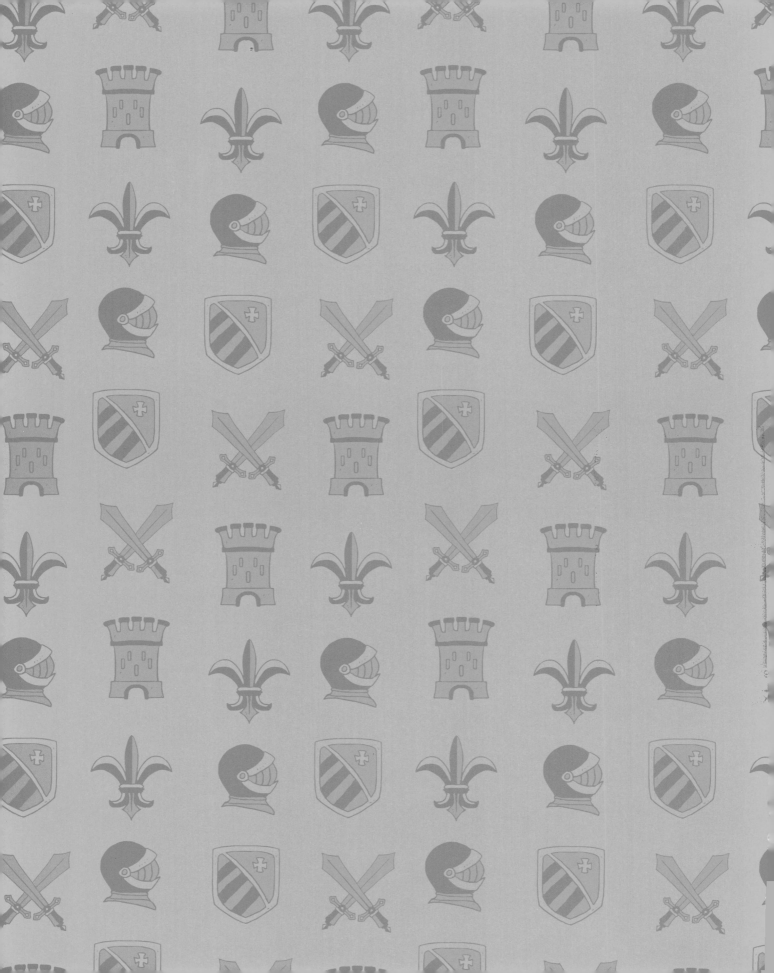